MW01119944

The Christmas Star

Abingdon Press
Nashville

The Christmas Star

by Denise Harris

ISBN 978-0-687-64746-0

09 10 11 12 13 14 15 16 17—10 9 8 7 6 5 4 3 2

Manufactured in the United States of America

Contents

Messengers and Messages

Scripture Reference: Luke 1:26-33; Genesis 6:13-22; Exodus 3:2-10; Exodus 5:1-2; Luke 1:46-47; Matthew 1:18-24; Luke 2:8-18

Characters: Narrator, Mary, the angel Gabriel, Noah, laughing and pointing people, Moses, Voice of God, Pharaoh, Joseph, Angels, Shepherds, modern-day people

Props: hammer and piece of wood for Noah, burning bush, throne for Pharaoh, cell phones

(Mary and Gabriel should be on stage without lights while Narrator is talking. Each time Narrator talks, the lights should be off while the next characters come on and the former ones leave.)

Narrator: In the days of Herod, there came an angel of the Lord to a young lady of the town of Galilee. Gabriel was the name of the angel. The message that Gabriel was sent to deliver was a message from God.

(Lights on.)

Gabriel: Hail Mary, the Lord is with thee. Blessed are thou among women.

Narrator: Mary, of course, was rather taken aback by these words. Who was she to be "blessed among women," and what was an angel doing in her room?

Gabriel: Fear not, Mary. You have found favor with the Lord. You will have a baby and his name shall be Jesus. And of his kingdom there will be no end.

(Lights dim. Gabriel and Mary leave, Noah comes out.)

Narrator: Now, just suppose that you are a young lady, engaged to be married to a man in your town, and an angel just told you that you are going to have a baby who is the Son of God. I don't know about you, but I think that message might be a bit unsettling. But if we really think about it, most messages from God were, to say the least, a bit unsettling. Take for instance the message Noah received:

(Lights on.)

Noah: *(as if repeating the words of God)* Go and make an ark of gopher wood, and fill it with two of every living species.

(Noah begins hammering—building the ark—in the middle of people laughing and pointing.)

Narrator: While Noah must have suffered ridicule from all those around him, he did as God asked.

(Lights dim and Noah leaves; Moses enters.)

Narrator: Moses' message came from a burning bush. A rather unusual way of sending a message—but nonetheless effective.

(Lights on. Moses kneels in front of burning bush as a booming voice orders:)

Voice of God: *(from offstage)* Go and bring my people to serve me on this mountain.

(Lights dim. Pharaoh comes out.)

Narrator: Moses did as God asked. He also served as God's messenger to Pharaoh:

(Lights on. Moses in front of Pharaoh, who is sitting on his throne)

Moses: Let my people go!

Narrator: Pharaoh had the unfortunate boldness to question not only Moses' message but also the source of the message.

Pharaoh: Who is this God that I should obey him? I know not this God!

(Lights dim. Mary comes back out and the others leave the stage.)

Narrator: Not a wise reply to say the least. All manners of plagues and misfortunes soon followed those foolish words. Speaking of obeying God, God gave us ten messages on two stone tablets brought down from the mountain by God's ever-faithful messenger, Moses. There is no misunderstanding a message (or should we say ten messages) when it is written in stone by God's own hand. But back to the angel standing in Mary's room. Mary recovered nicely from her shock and surprise. In words befitting the mother of Jesus, Mary answered:

(Lights on.)

Mary: My soul does magnify the Lord. And my spirit has rejoiced in my Savior.

(Lights dim. Joseph and an angel come out. Mary leaves.)

Narrator: Joseph did not rejoice, though, when he found out that the woman he was going to marry was with child. But Joseph, too, received a message from an angel. His angel messenger came to him in a dream.

(Lights on.)

Angel: *(appearing over a sleeping Joseph)* Do not be afraid to take Mary as your wife, Joseph. The baby is of the Holy Spirit.

6

(Lights dim. Angel and Joseph leave. Shepherds and Angels come out.)

Narrator: And then there were the shepherds. The shepherds were tending sheep in the fields when they got their message. Imagine being out in the field at night with sheep peacefully grazing. Then all of a sudden there's an angel in front of you.

(Lights on.)

Angel: *(talking to shepherds)* Do not be afraid, for I bring you good tidings of great joy. For there is born to you today, in the city of David, a Savior.

Narrator: Do not be afraid? I'm sure they were shaking in their sheepskin boots. Then as if one angel were not enough to scare even the most steadfast shepherd, a whole multitude of angels suddenly appeared. Their message was short and to the point.

Angels: Glory to God in the highest, and on earth peace, goodwill toward people!

(All earlier characters now come out on stage as the Narrator finishes. Then people with cell phones, talking and instant messaging, and someone singing all join crowd.)

(Crowd becomes quiet. Narrator comes on.)

Narrator: The shepherds left immediately for Bethlehem. Once they saw the newborn Savior, they became messengers for God. They told all around them what had been revealed to them.

This same message has been revealed to us and now we, like the shepherds, have been appointed as God's messengers. And in today's world, there are so many ways of sending messages. You can go high tech or low tech. You can send a letter. You can call someone on the phone with the message or you can text-message (just don't do it while driving, please). You can send an e-mail or an instant message. Word of mouth is still a great way of spreading a message as well as music, dance, and art.

So what exactly is the message we are trying to relay? Just go back to the beginning of this story. To the angel Gabriel and Mary: "You will have a Son and you will name him Jesus. And his Kingdom shall have no end!"

The Donkey's Tale

Scripture Reference: Luke 2:1-7; Mark 11:1-10

Characters: Donkey Dad, Donkey Son, Father Horse, Colt 1, Colt 2, Colt 3, Sheep, Cow

(Donkey Son stands out in the middle of three young horses [colts].)

Colt 1: Hey! Donkey! What do you use those big 'ole ears for? Do they wiggle when you giggle? Do they flap when you nap or when the wind blows? *(all three colts laughing)* Hey, I bet you can hear really well with those rabbit ears.

Colt 2: *(Coughs and says "freak" in the midst of a cough.)*

Colt 3: *(Sneezes and says "misfit" in the midst of a sneeze.)*

Colt 1: Hey, go back to the stable where you belong. Only us beautiful animals should be seen in the pasture.

(Donkey Son lowers head and walks away as Colts laugh. He walks to stable where Donkey Dad, Cow, and Sheep are standing.)

Donkey Dad: What's wrong, Son? Looks like all the clippity clop is gone from your step.

Donkey Son: It's the Colts again. They called me a freak and made fun of my ears. I've never done anything to them, Dad. Why do they have to be so mean?

Sheep: Don't listen to those Colts. Your ears don't look so baaaaad.

Cow: Of course they don't. Just tell those Colts to moooove away from you and leave you alone!

Donkey Dad: Sheep and Cow are right, Son. Just ignore the teasing. They probably don't know how important donkeys are and have been throughout history. Did I ever tell you the story about your great-great-great-great-grandfather?

Donkey Son: You mean great-great-grandpa Sunny? Is this another Grand Canyon story? How only we donkeys can navigate the roughest parts of the canyon? How horses don't even dare to go there?

Donkey Dad: No, not that one. This is far more important. It's all about a man named Jesus and the important role that our ancestors played in his life.

Donkey Son: Important role? A donkey?

Donkey Dad: Yes, a donkey! It all started when a man named Caesar Augustus ordered his fellow humans to go to the city of their ancestors for a census.

Donkey Son: What's a census?

Donkey Dad: A census is just a big word for a population count. Humans, for whatever reason, like to keep count of themselves. Anyway there was a young couple, Joseph and Mary, who had to travel from Nazareth to Bethlehem for the census.

Donkey Son: That shouldn't be a big deal. That's just like a three-day trip.

Donkey Dad: A three-day trip if you aren't about to have a baby!

Donkey Son: That might make the trip a bit more difficult. Surely great-great-great-great-grandpa just carried the lady when she got tired. And then when they all got to Bethlehem, she had a baby, they got counted, and they all lived happily ever after.

Donkey Dad: Not quite, Son. This was not just any baby that Mary was carrying. This was the Son of God.

Donkey Son: No way! Wouldn't God want one of those beautiful horses with small ears to carry Mary to Bethlehem?

Donkey Dad: I guess not. We were the chosen mounts. Yes, donkeys. And sure enough, your sure-footed great-great-great-great-grandfather was able to navigate the roads and keep Mary safe until they arrived in Bethlehem.

Donkey Son: So they arrived safely. I'm glad to hear that. Then Mary went to a nice house and had her baby, surrounded by all kinds of caring people.

Donkey Dad: Not quite, Son. There was no room at the inn. Mary and Joseph ended up going out to the stable with your great-great-great-great-grandfather and the other animals that were there.

Donkey Son: No way. She had to spend the night in a stable?

Donkey Dad: Not only did Mary spend the night in the stable, she had her baby in the stable.

Sheep: That's the truth. My great-great-great-great-grandparents say that they were left in their fields at night while their shepherds went to Baaathlehem to see the new King. Shepherds never leave their sheep out in the field. This was something very, very important.

Cow: My great-great-great-great-grandmother was in the stable when the baby was born. All the animals knew that something very special was happening. She said it was so mooooving to see that newborn baby.

Donkey Son: Wow. Wait till I tell the colts!

Donkey Dad: That's not all, Son. When Jesus was grown, guess who he chose as a mount to ride into Jerusalem?

Donkey Son: A beautiful stallion with a flowing mane and tail and short ears?

Cow: A chariot drawn by eight matching horses?

Sheep: I bet he chose a baaautiful Arabian horse with its shapely head held high as it pranced into Jerusalem as if walking on air.

Donkey Dad: No. You are all wrong. It was a donkey!

Donkey Son: Wow! Say, Dad, I'm going to go graze in the pasture a bit.

(Donkey Son goes out to the pasture. Soon he is surrounded by the Colts.)

Colt 1: Didn't we tell you that you were too ugly to graze with us?

Donkey Son: I thought you might like to hear a really neat story about the birth of Jesus, the Son of God, and how the mother of Jesus rode into Bethlehem on a donkey, and how a donkey was there when the Savior was born. I don't believe there were any horses, by the way.

Colt 1: But—but—there's no way that's true.

Father Horse: He's right, son. It was a donkey that brought Mary and Joseph to Bethlehem, and it was a donkey who was there at the birth of Jesus.

Colt 1: *(starts to say something else)* Buuuuu . . .

Donkey Son: Did you want to say something else?

Colt 1: *(shakes his head no)* Neigh.

A King Is Born

Scripture Reference: Luke 2:1-20; Matthew 2:1-11

Characters: Mary, Joseph, donkey, sheep, cows, shepherds, wise men, two-year-old Jesus, chorus of children

Props: manger, two chairs, doll for baby Jesus, cloth or towels for men's cloaks, cloth or towel for Mary's head-piece, crowns for wise men, gifts for wise men to give

Scene I

(Outside the stable. Mary, Joseph, and the donkey walk slowly toward the stable.)

Joseph: Come along, little donkey. Just a little longer. We are almost there. Inside we will surely find some hay for you. You can rest from our long journey.

(Joseph turns to Mary.)

Joseph: I know you must be very tired from our long journey. What an unfortunate time for us to have to travel to Bethlehem to be counted for the census.

Mary: Yes, I am tired, Joseph. I am so glad that the innkeeper found us a place to spend the night.

Donkey: Hee-haw! Hee-haw!

Joseph: *(gently opening the stable door)* Mary, this place will be perfect. We will be warm. Our precious baby will be safe.

Mary: *(smiling)* It won't be long now, Joseph. Soon Jesus will be here.

Sheep: Baa! Baa!

Cows: Moo! Moo!

Donkey: Hee-haw! Hee-haw!

Chorus of Children: A king is born! A king is born!

Scene II

(Inside the stable. Mary and Joseph sit in chairs beside the manger. The baby is in the manger.)

Mary: *(looking at the baby Jesus)* What a beautiful baby!

Joseph: *(looking at the baby Jesus)* Jesus is with us at last!

Sheep: Baa! Baa!

Cows: Moo! Moo!

Donkey: Hee-haw! Hee-haw!

Joseph: *(looking off in the distance)* Look, Mary. Someone is coming. We are going to have visitors.

Mary: *(smiling)* They have heard about the new baby. They have heard about the new king.

(Shepherds enter.)

Shepherds: *(kneeling beside Mary, Joseph, and the baby)* Angels came to us to tell us about this baby. What a beautiful king!

Mary: The baby's name is Jesus.

Chorus of Children: A king is born! A king is born!

Sheep: Baa! Baa!

Cows: Moo! Moo!

Donkey: Hee-haw! Hee-haw!

Scene III

(Inside a house. Mary and Joseph sit in chairs. Mary is holding two-year-old Jesus.)

Mary: *(looking off in the distance)* Oh, Joseph! Visitors are coming toward our home. Oh, my! They look like kings!

(Wise men enter.)

Joseph: *(motioning to the wise men to come closer)* Come in, friends. Come to see our baby. Come to see Jesus.

Wise Men: We are overwhelmed with joy!

Mary: Welcome. Come to see our son. His name is Jesus.

Wise Men: *(kneeling beside Mary, Joseph, and the baby)* We have watched the star for a long, long time. The star led us to you. We bring gifts to the baby king.

(Wise men hold out their gifts.)

Chorus of Children: A king is born! A king is born!

The Christmas Star

Scripture Reference: Luke 1:26-38; Luke 2:1-20

Characters: Mrs. Bush, Peter, Zach, Elizabeth, Innkeeper
non-speaking parts: Nathan, Tyronne, Jenna, Charise, Colby, Adam, a mother and her baby or a baby doll

Props: sheets of paper for scripts, manger

Act I

Mrs. Bush: Nathan, I've chosen you to be the donkey. Tyronne is the lamb, and Jenna is the cow. Shepherds are Charise, Colby, and Adam. Now, let's see about Joseph and Mary.

Peter: Please, Mrs. Bush, let me be Joseph.

Zach: No, I will make a better Joseph. Look, I have dark hair and dark eyes. Joseph wasn't blonde. Haven't you seen all those pictures of him?

Peter: Duh, those aren't pictures, those are paintings. They didn't have cameras back then.

Zach: I know that, but the paintings show what he would have looked like, and he was not blonde!

Mrs. Bush: Boys, boys. That will be quite enough. With all the arguing, I'll have to make you both Pharisees!

Zach: But brothers argue, Mrs. Bush. It's called sibling rivalry. Its biblical, too! Look at Cain and Abel, Jacob and Esau—

Peter: Drake and Josh—wait, that's Nickelodeon. But you know what we mean!

17

Mrs. Bush: "Love one another" is biblical, too. Those words came straight from Jesus' mouth. And since this is a play about Jesus, I think we'll abide by that biblical truth. Zach, you be Joseph. Peter, you are the angel Gabriel.

Peter: But Mrs. Bush, that's not fair. I'm being stereotyped as an angel because I have blonde hair. I want to be Joseph, I want to be the star of this play.

Zach: Sorry, brother, but there is only room for one star.

Mrs. Bush: To be perfectly honest, boys, neither of those parts is the starring role.

Peter: Well, who is the star, then? *(Zach lips the word* Joseph *to Peter and points to himself.)*

Mrs. Bush: Let's move on. Elizabeth, you be Mary. Okay, girls and boys. Here are your lines. *(Hands out papers.)* Rehearsal starts Sunday evening at 6:00 sharp.

(Curtain closes.)

Act II

(Curtain opens. All the young actors are assembled and ready for rehearsal. Zach and Peter immediately find Mrs. Bush.)

Zach: Mrs. Bush, Joseph only has a few lines.

Peter: Mrs. Bush, I, like, am only in the opening scene!

Mrs. Bush: Zach and Peter. This is not a competition. This is not a Broadway play. No agents will be scouting for future theatrical performers. I'm quite flattered that you think my drama is so important. It is, indeed—but not for the reasons you boys think. Now, let's start. Take your places, please.

(Mary is sitting in her room when Gabriel comes into the room.)

Peter as Gabriel: Fear not, Mary. You have found favor with God, and you are blessed among women. You shall bring forth a son and you shall name him Jesus. His kingdom will have no end.

Elizabeth as Mary: How can this be?

Peter as Gabriel: The Holy Spirit will come upon you. The one to be born is holy and will be called the Son of God.

Elizabeth as Mary: Let it be according to God's word.

(Angel departs. Audience of actors claps.)

Mrs. Bush: Great job, Peter and Elizabeth.

Peter: Yeah, actually I am quite good at the angel part.

Mrs. Bush: Okay. Scene two. Zach and Elizabeth, take your places.

Zach as Joseph: Mary, are you ready? I've packed everything.

Elizabeth as Mary: Oh, Joseph. I don't know if I can make that long trip.

Zach as Joseph: We have no choice. If you get too tired, I'll carry the provisions and the donkey can carry you. We'll make it, Mary. Three to four days and then we'll be there.

Mrs. Bush: Good, good. Now, the curtain will close here and when it opens again, you are almost to Bethlehem. You see an inn and stop to ask if there is any room.

Zach as Joseph: Look, Mary, I see Bethlehem.

Elizabeth as Mary: And not a moment too soon, Joseph. I believe tonight is the night.

Zach as Joseph: Let's stop here. *(knocking at an inn's door)* This looks like a fine place to stay.

Innkeeper: *(opening the door)* May I help you?

Zach as Joseph: Yes, we are in need of lodging. My wife is about to have a baby and we have been traveling for several days now.

Innkeeper: I'm so sorry. But the inn is full.

Zach as Joseph: Where else can we go to find lodging?

Innkeeper: Once again, I'm so sorry. All the inns and rooms for rent are full. The census has brought in travelers from all over. There is not even a closet that is empty. *(Innkeeper looks at Mary and shakes his head.)* All I have to offer is the stable. *(points to stable)*

Zach as Joseph: Thank you. *(Joseph looks in the direction of the stable and then back at Mary.)* The stable will have to do.

(Curtain closes. Actor audience claps.)

Zach: *(looking at Peter)* I told you I'd make a great Joseph.

Peter: And I made a great angel.

Zach: But I had more lines. That makes me the star.

Peter: I had the all-important message to deliver—that makes me the star.

Mrs. Bush: No, Zach and Peter. I hate to break this to you, but neither of you is the star. The star of this drama has no lines at all. Oh look! Here he comes now.

(A mother walks over with a baby and hands him to Elizabeth.)

Mrs. Bush: OK. Everyone take your places. *(Zach as Joseph, Elizabeth as Mary, the sheep, the cow, and the shepherds all gather around Mary. Beside Mary is a manger. The baby is in Mary's arms.)* Action! *(Immediately the shepherds fall to their knees. There is complete silence. Mary cradles the baby in her arms for several minutes and then rises slowly. Very carefully she places the baby in the manger.)*

(Curtain closes. Actor audience claps and cheers.)

Zach: Well, I guess we know who the star is now.

Peter: Yep, and he didn't even have to say a thing.

Zach: At last we agree! Hey, this isn't bad—we're not fighting. By the way, you did great as the angel.

Peter: You did great as Joseph.

Mrs. Bush: *(holding baby)* And you did great as the Christmas star!

Mi, Mi, Mi

Scripture Reference: Luke 2:1-20

Characters: Laura, Music Teacher, Brenna, Mary, Joseph, Innkeeper, shoppers, choir in play, audience watching play

Props: music stand/piano (for music lesson), wish list, pen or pencil, cell phone, bundle of straw, oil lamp, baby doll, swaddling cloth, manger

Scene I

(Teacher and student are in a voice lesson.)

Laura: *(singing)* Do, re, mi—Oh, I love that one! It reminds me of Christmas. *(singing)* Me, me, me. I can't wait. What will Santa bring me? What will mom and dad buy me? Not to mention grandmom and granddad. Aunts and uncles. Friends. Did I mention that I want . . .

Music Teacher: Yes, yes, Laura. I've heard all about you and what you want for Christmas. How Christmas is your favorite holiday and how you are going to get lots and lots of gifts under that Christmas tree. If I didn't know better, I would think that Christmas is all about you.

Laura: Well, that's not a bad idea, actually! All about me. *(looks at her watch)* Well thank you, Mrs. Smith. I've got to go shopping now. Well, not really shopping—I'm going Christmas wish-list making. Time to look around and make out my Christmas list. *(reaches into purse and pulls out a piece of paper that then falls open revealing a really long paper)* Gee, I don't have enough room.

Music Teacher: That's what they said at the inn. *(shakes her head)*

Laura: What's that, Mrs. Smith?

Music Teacher: Oh, nothing. I was just thinking about the real meaning of Christmas. You probably won't believe this, Laura, but it's not all about you. The meaning of Christmas has been distorted and commercialized. The name of the holiday is under attack, and the gift given that very special day—while still given year in and year out—is so often rejected or forgotten.

Laura: What are you talking about, Mrs. Smith? What gift are you talking about?

Music Teacher: My point exactly.

Laura: Wait, hold on, I've got to text-message Marshall. He wants to know what I want for Christmas. *(sends a text message on her phone)* What were you saying?

Music Teacher: I'm just hoping that you'll find the true meaning of Christmas one day.

Laura: Sure, Mrs. Smith. I'll do it right after I'm done with my shopping.

(Curtain closes.)

Scene II

(Curtain opens on department store bustling with shoppers. Laura is walking through the store writing things on her list. She sees her friend Brenna.)

Laura: Brenna! Hey! *(They hug.)* Are you making your wish list too?

Brenna: No, I'm buying gifts for a little girl who is on the Angel Wings list.

Laura: That's nice. Now tell me what you're getting or at least hoping to get!

Brenna: I really don't need anything. To be honest, I've got too much already. This year I'm asking my parents and family to take some of the money they would spend on me and give it to the needy.

Laura: No, really . . . you're serious?

Brenna: Hey, why don't you come to my church with me tonight? My sister is in the Christmas play.

Laura: *(looks at her list and then looks at her friend)* Why not? I can make my list at home. Will they be serving refreshments after the play?

Brenna: *(laughing)* Of course.

Laura: *(dialing cell phone and talking as the two walk off stage)* Mom, I'm going to the Christmas play with Brenna tonight if that's okay with you.

(Curtain closes.)

Scene III

(Curtain opens.)

(Audience, including Laura and Brenna, is gathered around to watch Christmas play. Joseph and Mary are walking down the road and stop at an inn. Joseph knocks. Nobody answers. They stop and look at each other.)

Mary: Joseph, what if they don't have room for us here, either? I'm not sure that I can go any farther. I'm cold, and Joseph, I think it's almost time. *(Joseph knocks with more urgency.)*

Innkeeper: *(voice from behind the door)* I'm coming, I'm coming! Everyone's in such a hurry these days. *(opens the door and looks at the couple)*

Joseph: Good evening, sir. We were looking for a place to stay. Everywhere we've stopped is full, and my wife is about to have a baby.

Innkeeper: *(His face softens and he smiles.)* A baby! I sure wish I could help you but there is no room here, either.

Joseph: But you have to help us. My wife just can't go any farther.

Innkeeper: I do have a stable. It's not much, but it will at least shield you from the wind. *(points to stable)* I'm sorry, but that's all I have to offer. Wait a minute, though. *(turns and picks up items)* Take this bundle of straw and this oil lamp.

Joseph: Well, we're thankful for anything at this point. We will spend the night in your stable.

(Joseph and Mary walk off the stage. Lights dim so that the manger scene can be set up.)

Laura: *(talking to Brenna)* Why were all the inns full? Surely there weren't that many people traveling back in those days.

Brenna: Well, usually not. But Caesar Augustus sent out a decree that all the world should be enrolled. That meant that he was taking a census and that Jews from all over had to come to their ancestral homes and be counted. This meant that Joseph and Mary would have to travel from Nazareth to Bethlehem. This is why there were so many people traveling and the inns and private homes were all filled. The stable that the innkeeper was talking about was probably a cave stable. Caves were great shelter for the livestock back then.

Laura: Wow, you know a lot about this.

(*Lights brighten. Joseph is bending over the baby as Mary wraps Jesus in swaddling cloth. Choir in the background is singing "Away in a Manger." When singing stops, Mary speaks.*)

Mary: Yes, Jesus is a beautiful name. We shall call him Jesus.

Joseph: I will go to register. You rest. When you feel able to travel, we will go back home.

(*Lights dim, indicating the end of the Christmas play. Laura and Brenna are leaving.*)

Laura: Wow, you mean Jesus the Son of God was born under those horrible circumstances? They didn't even have a house to stay in, much less heaters or running water or—cell phones!

Brenna: That's right. Our Savior, Jesus, didn't come riding in on a fantastic steed with an army of angels behind him. He came as a tiny baby. No fanfare, no hurrah, no place even to stay but a stable. Yet his coming was our gift of salvation. And every Christmas we celebrate that gift.

Laura: Oh, boy. I'm embarrassed. Every Christmas I celebrate my gifts, but it's been a long time since I've included that one among them. Is it too late—I mean after all these years of worrying about all the other gifts I'm going to get—can I still accept God's gift?

Brenna: Of course you can. That gift is endless. God's love for us is endless. All we have to do is accept it. Nothing to sign, no contracts, no negotiating, no strings attached.

Laura: You better believe I'm going to accept it. So what happens next? They go back to Nazareth where Jesus grows up?

Brenna: Not exactly. Actually they have to flee to Egypt to keep baby Jesus safe from King Herod. Remember when the wise men were invited to see King Herod on their way to find the baby Jesus?

Laura: Not exactly.

Brenna: *(puts arm around Laura's shoulders)* Don't worry. I'll tell you about that, too. That's a whole other story! *(Curtain closes as Brenna starts telling about the three wise men.)* There were these wise men . . .

(Curtain closes.)

Angel Whispers

Scripture Reference: Luke 2:8-20

Characters: Celeste (angel), 6 other angels, shepherds and sheep (as many as desired), Mary, Joseph, voice of crying baby

Props: harps and other instruments, manger, baby doll

Note: This is a great drama for younger children, as the speaking parts for the angels are very simple. You can include many other children as shepherds and sheep, and two more as Mary and Joseph.

Scene I

(Angels 1-5 are playing instruments or singing or clapping. Small children can lip-synch music. Celeste claps along with other angels.)

Narrator: Heaven was exploding with excitement. Angels from all over were coming together to practice their best lullabies and songs. Harps were sounding, bells were ringing, an endless number of angels was singing. The air danced with beautiful music. Sitting among this large gathering of angels was Celeste. Celeste was a very soft-spoken angel. Her voice was barely loud enough to be heard. In fact, at its loudest, Celeste's voice was just a whisper, but it was a beautiful whisper.

Angel 6: *(running in toward group of angels)* It's time, it's time!

(All the angels except Celeste run over to Angel 6.)

Angel 1: Let's go, angels!

Angel 2: To the fields!

Angel 3: To tell the shepherds!

Angel 4: Tidings of great joy!

Angel 5: *(looks over at Celeste, who is still sitting)* Are you not coming, Celeste?

Celeste: *(in a whisper)* You all go on. No one will hear my whispers.

Angels 1-4: *(all together)* What?

Angel 5: She said for us to go on, that no one will hear her whispers.

(Angels leave the stage, except for Celeste.)

(Curtain closes.)

Scene II

Narrator: The other angels left in the blink of an eye. They passed the king's magnificent castle. They passed the holy temples built with gold, silver, and precious jewels. They went to the fields to find the people chosen to receive such important news. They went to the shepherds tending their sheep.

(Curtain opens and angels are talking to shepherds with their sheep.)

Angel 1: I bring you good news!

Angel 2: A Savior was born today in the city of Bethlehem.

Angels 3-6: Glory to God and on earth, peace and goodwill to people!

(The shepherds go running from the stage shouting, "Good news! Good news!")

(Curtain closes.)

Scene III

Narrator: When the shepherds heard the news, they left their sheep and set out to see the baby Jesus. Back in Bethlehem, though, all was not well. The night was clear and the stable cold, and the baby Jesus was softly crying. The angels watched from heaven.

(Curtain opens. Baby is crying. Mary is holding baby, then hands him to Joseph, who walks with him trying to comfort him. All angels are watching at the side of the stage.)

Angel 6: We have to do something.

Angel 1: Think! How can we help?

Angel 2: I have an idea! We can sing lullabies.

Angel 3: I can play the harp.

Angel 4: Then Jesus will surely sleep.

Angel 5: Like a baby!

Angel 6: Celeste! Do come with us!

Angels 1-6: *(All the angels encourage Celeste to come.)* Yes, come with us!

Celeste: Yes, I will come!

(Curtain closes.)

Scene IV

Narrator: At the stable, the angels gathered at the foot of the manger.

(Curtain opens. Angels 1-6 are gathered at foot of manger, singing a lullaby or lip-synching with music.)

Narrator: *(when song is finished)* With heavenly voices, they sang the sweetest lullabies that had ever been sung, and yet the baby Jesus continued to cry.

Angel 1: Harps! Let's play the harps.

(Angels grab their harps. Children can act like they are playing harps with or without actual music.)

Narrator: The sound of angelic harps filled the air with the loveliest melodies ever heard, but still the baby cried. Then Celeste spoke in what was, for Celeste, a rather loud voice.

Celeste: *(loud whisper)* Let me try! *(Celeste goes over to the manger and starts whispering to the baby Jesus.)*

Narrator: Celeste gently leaned over and whispered in Jesus' ear. She told him of God's love, in a whisper sweet and clear. And the baby Jesus was soon fast asleep.

(Crying suddenly stops. All the other angels look at each other in surprise.)

Angels: *(to each other)* How did she do that? I don't know. What happened? What did she say?

Angel 4: What did you whisper, Celeste?

Angel 3: What words could have comforted him so much?

Angel 2: Yes, we want to know!

Celeste: *(smiling)* I simply told him how much God loves him!

Narrator: From that time on, whenever baby Jesus cried, special angels sent by God would whisper at his side. For more beautiful than the singing of angels, more lovely than the melody of heavenly harps, are angel whispers telling of God's endless love!

Westward Bound

Scripture Reference: Matthew 2:1-12

Characters: Narrator, 3 Wise Men, Herod, 2 Scribes, Choir

Props: food and drink for wise men, satchel, map

Act I

Narrator: The night sky is full of stars but only once did this special star shine. It prompted three men of great knowledge to set out on a long and difficult journey. These three were from the Orient, a land far east of Bethlehem. They were very scholarly men who studied the stars. Through their knowledge of the stars these men knew that the time of the Savior had come. They were now westward bound on a journey to find and worship the new King of the Jews.

(Curtain opens, revealing three wise men on their journey.)

Choir: *(Sing first verse of "We Three Kings.")*

First Wise Man: We are close. The star is growing ever brighter with each step that we take.

Second Wise Man: You are surely right. Let's hurry; we are so close.

Third Wise Man: I, too, am excited, but we should stop at Jerusalem and rest. We have traveled long, and we need more food and water. By my calculations, we are just half a day from Jerusalem.

First Wise Man: Yes, we will stop and rest in Jerusalem. Then we will proceed to where the star is leading us.

(Curtain closes.)

Act II

Narrator: King Herod heard that men from the east had come into Jerusalem and were asking about the Messiah. This news disturbed the king. He called together all of the chief priests and scribes, who knew the prophecies and might be able to tell him the purpose of this visit.

(Curtain opens, revealing Herod and the scribes.)

Scribe 1: It is written that a Messiah, a King of the Jews, will be born.

Herod: Where will the Messiah be born?

Scribe 2: The prophets have written that from Bethlehem will come a leader to guide the people of Israel.

Herod: Find our wise visitors from the East, and bring them to me. Bring them here secretly.

(Scribes leave.)

Choir: *(Sing to tune of "Did You Ever See a Lassie?")*

> Go and summon these three men of great knowledge, great knowledge.
> Go and summon these three men, and bring them to me.
> For I need to know where to find the child Savior.
> Go and summon these three men, and bring them to me.

(Wise men enter.)

Herod: *(to the wise men)* Come in and be my guests. Your journey has been long, and I wish to welcome you.

Second Wise Man: Yes, we have traveled far, and we are in need of food and rest.

Herod: Eat, drink. You need strength to continue on in search of the Christ child. I, too, am looking for this child. I ask only one favor. When you find him, return to me and tell me where he is so that I may go and worship him, too.

Narrator: *(while wise men and Herod are visiting in the background)* The wise men ate and drank and enjoyed Herod's hospitality, not realizing that this was all an evil plan on the part of Herod to find out where the child Jesus was. Herod had no intention of worshiping Jesus. He intended to kill him. Herod was not the rightful heir to the throne of Israel, and Herod was afraid he would lose all of his power because of this new King.

First Wise Man: *(as all three are about to leave)* Certainly. We will be glad to bring you news of the Child.

(Wise men go offstage.)

Choir: *(Sing to tune of "Baa Baa Black Sheep.")*

> Onward, wise men, to the baby King
> Gold and myrrh and frankincense you bring
> Follow, follow, follow yonder star
> Shining brightly, now it isn't far
> Onward, wise men, to the baby King
> Gold and myrrh and frankincense you bring.

(Curtain closes.)

Act III

Narrator: The wise men left in search of the child. The star went ahead of the wise men and stopped over the place where Jesus was. The wise men went in to see this new King. They fell upon their knees and offered the Holy Child their gifts of gold, frankincense, and myrrh!

(Curtain opens. Wise men are all sleeping.)

First Wise Man: *(jumps up from sleeping)* Wake up! I have had a dream. It was an angel of the Lord telling me not to return home by way of Jerusalem. We must not, under any circumstances, let King Herod know about Jesus or where the family is staying!

Second Wise Man: *(takes out map from satchel)* I will find another route. We must leave immediately.

(Wise men leave the stage.)

Choir: *(Sing to tune of "London Bridge.")*

> Go back home another way. Choose a route. Leave today.
> News of Jesus do not bring—to King Herod.

Narrator: The wise men left immediately. They chose another route home. King Herod never did find the Christ child—but those truly wise people did—and still do!

(Curtain closes.)

CHRISTMAS in One Word

Scripture Reference: Luke 2:1-20; Matthew 1:18-24; Matthew 2:1-16

Characters: nine speakers

Props: nine large sheets of paper or posterboard, each printed with a different letter in the word *Christmas*

(The speakers will come out on stage in the correct order, holding their letters. Each will tell part of the Christmas story with a word beginning with the letter she or he is holding.)

C: Caesar Augustus. Caesar Augustus, the ruler of the Roman Empire, ordered a census. This meant everyone had to go to the home of their ancestors to be counted. Ancestors are grandparents and great-grandparents and great-great-grandparents and so on. Joseph's ancestors were from Bethlehem, from the line of King David. Mary and Joseph would have to travel to Bethlehem. This trip would be difficult since Mary was about to have a baby.

H: Herod. These were the days of Herod, the king of Judea. Herod heard rumors about the child Savior. Herod was afraid. He was afraid that he would no longer be the king. Herod was always worried. He was worried that someone would take over his throne. He was especially worried about the baby Jesus. Herod was a horrible man and an unjust ruler who was appointed by the Romans.

R: Righteous. Being a righteous man, Joseph intended to leave Mary when he found out that she was with child. But Joseph was a good man and did not want to publicly shame Mary. He decided to send her away quietly. Instead, an angel came to Joseph in a dream and assured Joseph that the child to be born was the Son of God. Joseph then knew how special Mary truly was.

I: Inn. The journey was long, Mary was tired, and there was no room in the inn. Usually there would be plenty of lodging in and around Bethlehem, but the census brought travelers to Bethlehem from all over. All the inns were full. There was no room for Mary and Joseph.

S: Stable. Jesus was born in a stable. Not in a palace or mansion. Just a lowly stable. Mary wrapped him in swaddling cloth and laid him in a manger. The Savior's coming was expected. It was foretold in many writings. Most people, though, expected a hero of epic strength to come and save the day, a prince who would come and take what was his, by force if necessary. Instead, they received a baby. A baby who would grow to be as unassuming as his birthplace surroundings.

T: Tidings of Great Joy! That is what the angels brought to the shepherds out in the field tending their flocks at night. The first people invited to see Jesus were shepherds—men of little importance by the standards of that time period. The shepherds went and beheld the baby, and they made known to all who would listen what they had seen.

M: Magi. Magi, or wise men, from the far east made their way to Bethlehem. They brought with them treasures for the newborn King. These men were most likely astronomers. They studied astrology and followed the star. The star guided them on their journey. The three wise men were wealthy, splendidly dressed and riding camels. They were welcomed when they arrived to see Jesus. The shepherds, on the other hand, were poor men of simple dress walking on foot. How interesting that they were the ones invited to see Jesus.

A: Angel. An angel warned the wise men in a dream not to return to Herod with the news of Jesus. The wise men chose another route home that did not include Jerusalem. When Herod finally figured out that he had been tricked, he flew into a rage and ordered the death of every male child in Bethlehem born within the past two years.

S: Savior. This is the reason for Christmas—to celebrate the birth of our Savior Jesus. A savior, born in a manger. Meager beginnings to say the least. The beginning, the middle, and the end of Jesus' life share a common theme. They all reflect an attitude of humility and servitude. Most of us go through life taking all we can from it. Jesus, though, showed us a different way—to go through life giving all we can to it.

Christmas. One day. One word. One Savior.

All Is Wonderful, All Is Well

Baby Jesus born today
In a manger filled with hay.
Angels from the heavens sing
Joyful, joyful news they bring.

Special baby, special night.
Shepherds bathed in angel light,
Sent to see the newborn King.
Joyful, joyful news they bring.

Little Jesus, fast asleep
Safe now in his Father's keep.
Angel whispers sweetly tell
All is wonderful, all is well.

Coming and Going

When I was a young child, Christmas was a time
     of great excitement:
Gifts were coming! Gifts from family and friends.
Gifts from classmates and Sunday school teachers.
Gifts in beautiful packages with brightly colored ribbons
     and bows.
And when all the gifts were opened, the joy of receiving
     was so very satisfying.
And the joy lasted for several weeks until the toys were
     no longer new and exciting.

Now that I am older, Christmas is still a time
     of great excitement:
Gifts are going! Gifts for family and friends.
Gifts for children who otherwise wouldn't receive gifts.
Gifts in beautiful packages and brightly colored ribbons
     and bows.
And when all the gifts are opened, the joy of giving
     is so very satisfying.
And the joy of giving lasts long past the joy of the gift itself!

Few things in life last like the joy of giving gifts
     and the joy of receiving God's special gift of Jesus.

Five Pretty Presents!

Five pretty presents stacked upon the floor,
(Make stacking motions.)

Tear one open and then there are four.
(Make tearing motions.)

Four pretty presents below the Christmas tree,
(Point to the ground, then make tree shape over head.)

Tear one open and then there are three.
(Make tearing motions.)

Three pretty presents with ribbons green and blue,
(Make ribbon-tying motions.)

Tear one open and then there are two.
(Make tearing motions.)

Two pretty presents that promise lots of fun,
(Wave arms above head and smile big.)

Tear one open and then there is one.
(Make tearing motions.)

One special present left! Can you guess?
(Make the number 1 with index finger.)

A gift from God to all: J E S U S!
(Sign the word Jesus while spelling the letters.)

To sign the word Jesus,
touch the middle finger of the right hand
to the palm of the left hand, then
reverse.

The Deep Desert Sand

Over the dunes and the deep desert sand
And into a grassy, faraway land,
The three men continued to search far and wide,
With only a star in the sky as their guide.

They rode upon camels, these three men so bold,
And brought with them frankincense, myrrh, and pure gold.
They wore costly robes never seen in this land,
These three men who crossed o'er the deep desert sand.

Jerusalem, Bethlehem, where could he be,
This King of the Jews that they traveled to see?
They stopped by King Herod's and asked did he know—
Where this child lived, to which town should they go?

The king quickly answered, "You must look some more.
Go on to Bethlehem, search door to door.
If you should find him, then bring back the news.
I want to honor this King of the Jews."

The three men kept searching and then one dark night,
They saw a small house underneath the star's light.
A child played inside while his mother sat near.
At last they had found him, God's own Son so dear.

They opened their treasure and knelt down in joy
To honor the child, this most wonderful boy.
They gave him their gifts and when they were done,
They thanked God for sending God's own special Son.

Later that night they were warned not to bring
News of the Christ child to Herod the king.
They chose a new way to return to their land,
These three men who crossed o'er the deep desert sand.

Advent Worship

The Advent wreath is a simple circle of evergreen branches, which is a sign of life without end. Four purple Advent candles encircle a central white Christ candle. Each Sunday of Advent one additional purple candle is lighted until all four are lighted. On Christmas Eve and Day, the middle white Christ candle is lighted, and all the candles are burning.

First Sunday of Advent

LEADER: This is the first Sunday of the church season we call Advent. Advent is a time when we wait and get ready to celebrate the birth of the Savior. The Savior is Jesus.

READER 1: We light the first candle of Advent. Today we light the candle of HOPE. The prophet Isaiah told God's people to have hope. A Savior was coming. That Savior was baby Jesus. *(Light the first purple candle.)*

READER 2: *(Read Luke 1:30-32.)*

ALL: *(Sing "O Come, O Come, Emmanuel.")*

CHILDREN: Thank you, God, for sending baby Jesus.

LEADER: Thank you, God, for sending Jesus, our Savior. Fill us with hope. Amen.

Second Sunday of Advent

LEADER: Today is the second Sunday of Advent. This is the second of four Sundays when we prepare for the birth of Jesus. *(Light the first two purple candles.)*

READER 1: The first candle is the candle of HOPE. God gave the people hope with the promise of a Savior.

READER 2: The second candle is the candle of LOVE. Jesus was God's gift of love to the whole world.

READER 1: *(Read Luke 2:6-7.)*

ALL: *(Sing "Love Came Down at Christmas.")*

CHILDREN: Thank you, God, for sending baby Jesus.

LEADER: Dear God, we thank you for the prophets who told the people to have hope. We thank you for your loving gift of our Savior. Help us to be hopeful and share the love of Jesus as we prepare to celebrate Christmas. Amen.

Third Sunday of Advent

LEADER: Today is the third Sunday of the season of Advent. *(Light the first three purple candles.)*

READER 1: The first candle is the candle of HOPE. God gave the people hope with the promise of a Savior.

READER 2: The second candle is the candle of LOVE. Jesus was God's gift of love to the whole world.

READER 1: The third candle is the candle of JOY. The angels told the shepherds about the joyful birth.

READER 2: *(Read Luke 2:10-11.)*

ALL: *(Sing "Joy to the World.")*

CHILDREN: Thank you, God, for sending baby Jesus.

LEADER: Dear God, we thank you for the prophets who told the people to have hope. We thank you for your loving gift of our Savior. We thank you for the joy that Jesus brought to the world. Help us to be hopeful and filled with love as we share the joyful news. Amen.

Fourth Sunday of Advent

LEADER: Today is the fourth Sunday of the season of Advent. *(Light all four purple candles.)*

READER 1: The first candle is the candle of HOPE. God gave the people hope with the promise of a Savior.

READER 2: The second candle is the candle of LOVE. Jesus was God's gift of love to the whole world.

READER 1: The third candle is the candle of JOY. The angels told the shepherds about the joyful birth.

READER 2: The fourth candle is the candle of PEACE. God sent Jesus to be the Prince of Peace.

READER 1: *(Read Luke 2:14.)*

ALL: *(Sing "Silent Night.")*

CHILDREN: Thank you, God, for sending baby Jesus.

LEADER: Dear God, we thank you for the prophets who gave the people hope. We thank you for Jesus, your gift of love to the world. We thank you for the angels, who announced the joyful birth. We thank you for the child who came to bring us peace. Amen.

Christmas Day

LEADER: The time of waiting is over. We have been waiting to celebrate the birth of Jesus, and it has finally come. *(Light the four purple candles.)*

READER 1: The first candle is the candle of HOPE. God gave the people hope with the promise of a Savior.

READER 2: The second candle is the candle of LOVE. Jesus was God's gift of love to the whole world.

READER 1: The third candle is the candle of JOY. The angels told the shepherds about the joyful birth.

READER 2: The fourth candle is the candle of PEACE. God sent Jesus to be the Prince of Peace.

READER 1: The Christ candle celebrates the birth of Jesus, the Son of God. *(Light the white Christ candle.)*

READER 2: *(Read Isaiah 9:6.)*

ALL: *(Sing "Away in a Manger.")*

CHILDREN: Thank you, God, for sending baby Jesus.

LEADER: Thank you, God, for the gift of Jesus, who brings us hope, love, joy, and peace. Amen.

Prayers for Christmas

Loving God,
We thank you for sending Jesus, the promised Messiah. You said he would be our Wonderful Counselor. From his life and example, we know your love for us. We know you are with us in all times and places. Thank you for the difference that one precious baby has made in our lives. Amen.

Dear God,
Thank you for your Son, Jesus. Thank you for sending him to show us what you are like. Jesus' birth proves that your love is for all people. Help us to share your love as we love one another. Thank you, God, that your love is for me. Amen.

Dear God,
Please be with us. Help us to slow down and remember what these days of Advent and Christmas are all about. Help us to focus on the One who came to save us. Help us to rejoice in the love you have given us through your Son. We love you, and we thank you. Amen.

Perfect God,
We thank you for your Son, Jesus. You knew the perfect time to send Jesus, our promised Messiah. Please send your Holy Spirit to help us to have faith and patience that is strong. Help us to know that you know the perfect time for all things to happen. Amen.